MY JOURNEY

By
Spiros Kalampalikis

Order this book online at www.trafford.com/06-2818
or email orders@trafford.com

Most Trafford titles are also available at major online book retailers.

Printed in Victoria, BC, Canada.

ISBN: 978-1-4251-1059-8

*We at Trafford believe that it is the responsibility of us all, as both individuals
and corporations, to make choices that are environmentally and socially sound.
You, in turn, are supporting this responsible conduct each time you purchase a
Trafford book, or make use of our publishing services. To find out how you are
helping, please visit www.trafford.com/responsiblepublishing.html*

*Our mission is to efficiently provide the world's finest, most comprehensive
book publishing service, enabling every author to experience success.
To find out how to publish your book, your way, and have it available
worldwide, visit us online at www.trafford.com/10510*

www.trafford.com

North America & international
toll-free: 1 888 232 4444 (USA & Canada)
phone: 250 383 6864 ♦ fax: 250 383 6804
email: info@trafford.com

The United Kingdom & Europe
phone: +44 (0)1865 722 113 ♦ local rate: 0845 230 9601
facsimile: +44 (0)1865 722 868 ♦ email: info.uk@trafford.com

10 9 8 7 6 5

Dedication

To my devoted wife Darlene who supported and encouraged me to finish my book.

To my parents: Elias and Paraskevi Kalampalikis.

To my siblings: Nicholas, Tom, Konstantia, Lazaros, and Miltiadis Kalampalikis.

Acknowledgements

I would like to thank my parents: Elias and Paraskevi Kalampalikis, who through their struggles to raise their six children in the storm of wars, showed us how to love, respect and to appreciate everything in our lives.

To my lovely wife, a special "thank you for your advice, support and understanding".

I would like to thank my brothers: Nicholas, Tom, Lazaros, Miltiadis, my sister: Konstantia and many family members, who supported me and supplied me with material for my book.

A special thank you goes to my nephews: Anestis Kalampalikis, Christos Kalampalikis, Aristidis Kalampalikis and Ilias Kalampalikis for their encouragement to finish this book.

I would like to thank my niece Angeliki Bolgoura Kalampalikis, who typed my story, corrected all my errors and readied my material to be translated to English.

A very warm thank you to Dr. Niki Karavasilis for her guidance in getting this book completed. Without her help this book would never have come to fruition.

Preface

My journey is long and the reader will be faced with my daily struggles of survival in the midst of war, starvation, and my experiences in a new land; the United States of America.

I never gave up. However, I knew deep down in my heart, I had received the best foundation from my parents to succeed in life. They always taught me to work hard, to do my best, to live life to its fullest and to love my family and my friends.

I have lived a rich life. I was fortunate to live in two beautiful countries: Greece and America. Two wonderful civilizations!

I reaped the fruit of both lands, although sometimes it was hard to face the everyday life without knowing the English language and not being acquainted with the new customs. Over all, it has been an enjoyable journey.

MY JOURNEY

The village of Argiri

This is my story. A story of difficulties, successes, love for my beloved wife, my parents, siblings, my native country, Greece, and my adoptive country, the United States of America.

My name is Spiros Kalampalikis. I was born on January 11, 1927, in a very small village called Argiri, not very far from Karditsa, the big city in Thessali, the central part of Greece,. It is a beautiful and religious village surrounded by four churches: Saint Nicholas, Saint Athanasios, the Assumption of Virgin Mary, and the Prophet Ilias. This is the village where my parents Ilias and Paraskevi Kalampalikis lived and had five boys and a girl.

I began to feel the punches of life ever since I was three and a half years old. I remember my beloved mother breastfeeding me up to the age of four. In the summer time, we lived in Prava, a section of Argiri where we cultivated the land. We lived in a small house, which had a balcony that was ten feet high. We had a small kitten. One day, I tried to throw it down from the balcony, but somehow, she managed to hold on to my chest and both of us landed below the balcony. I started to cry. My poor mother, full of fear, ran to see what had happened. She found the two of us underneath the balcony; kitten and small Spiro, unharmed.

It was in 1932, at the age of five that I started the first grade. My teacher's name was George Papathanasiou who was born in Argiri. He was a priest and a teacher of the village. It was common at that time for one to execute two professions at the same time. My first year in school was difficult for me as I was shy. When the second year came around, school became enjoyable and entertaining for me, especially when we played games during recess. I played constantly until nighttime. I would go to bed exhausted and hungry. In the morning when I woke up, I was starving and ready to eat the breakfast that my mother had already prepared. My brother Nicholas was older than I, and was born in 1923. He was my protector and my closest friend during my childhood.

School of Argiri

In school, I was very good in history, geography and religion, but not good in Math. The school was small and consisted of thirty-five boys. Girls didn't attend school back then. They stayed home, and learned to cook, embroider and many other household chores.

The months were passing by quickly and before I knew it, winter had arrived and the whole village was covered in fluffy white powder. A severe cold engulfed the small village of Argiri. Life was getting hard, especially when it was time to go to school. The big school building had no heating system except for the woodstove in the middle of the large classroom. Every day it was the responsibility of all the students to bring a log for the woodstove in order to heat the freezing classroom. I never liked winter ever since I was a small child. I felt uncomfortable having to stay indoors all day long due to the severe winds, without the freedom of going outside. I preferred spring when the trees had blossomed and wild flowers adorned the hills of the village, spreading their aroma everywhere. Summer was also another favorite season of mine, with the abundance of fruit, stringing along autumn with the gathering of the corn, grapes and the delicious figs.

Our village was very poor. It had a population of two hundred people. The inhabitants were stock-farmers and produced the potent liquor called *"tsipouro"* from grapes, and just enough wheat and corn for survival. Transportation didn't exist. Mules and donkeys were used to go to Mouzaki and Arta to shop for different items. There was one telephone in the village for emergencies, but in the wintertime, that too didn't function due to winter and heavy snowstorms.

In 1931, my sister Kostantia was born. Four years went by after her birth, and my brother Tom came along into our family in 1935. My family was getting larger and larger as the years came and went. It seemed to me that God was giving us children for gifts instead of the comforts of life.

In 1936, Mr. Papathanasiou, the teacher, left the village and went to Farsala, Thessali. We got a new teacher who didn't stay for long, since our village was very poor and didn't offer anything exciting. New teachers didn't stay at the Mouzaki High School for long. They always asked for a transfer to the bigger villages and cities. In two years, we had three teachers: Geroukis, Mamalis and Athanasios Dermatas. The constant change of teachers was detrimental to all the students.

I finished the grammar school in 1938 with the final mark seven. Ten was the highest. There was no money for me to attend. The same thing happened to my brother Nicholas, who stayed in the village and went to Mr. Theofani Tsirogiani to learn the trade of a cobbler.

It was a beautiful autumn day. The leaves were changing into different colors and the breeze was embracing all the corners of the village. I was sitting quietly in the courtyard observing nature, when suddenly my father told me we would be going to Mouzaki soon to meet Mr. Christo Petarouda, the tailor. "You are going to learn to be a tailor, a trade you like so much," he said. I was thrilled! I always loved that occupation and I could not wait to go to Mouzaki to meet Mr. Petarouda. I remember so clearly that special day. It was at the end of September when my father and I started our journey to Mouzaki. We walked for many hours. I was making plans all along the way of how great a tailor I was going to be in the future. After many agonizing hours of walking, we finally arrived at our destination. We didn't lose any time and we headed for the house of Mr. Petarouda. He was going to be my boss and master of my trade. My father introduced me to him. I observed him from top to bottom to find out if I was going to like him or not. I waited! My future was before me, but when my father asked him what it would take to teach me to become a tailor, Mr. Petarouda answered, "In order for me to teach your son this trade, you have to pay me 60 okathes of wheat per month". I was shocked that Mr. Petarouda was asking for so many pounds of wheat and I waited for my father's answer: "I don't have enough wheat to feed my family, and it would be impossible for me to come up with so much wheat for this trade. I thank you for taking the time to talk to us." My future plans of becoming a famous tailor melted before my eyes. We did not have enough wheat to pay Mr. Petarouda to teach me to be a tailor. We returned to the village, a father and a disappointed son, who would never have the opportunity to become a *famous tailor.*

I was devastated at not having enough money to learn the trade. I would see the other children who were well dressed in beautiful clothes and new shoes, and would be ashamed that we didn't have nice clothing. I knew full well that my parents didn't have any money because our family was big, the village was very poor and we didn't produce a lot of food. I loved my parents and I respected them. My father never hit me and my mother slapped my face when I did something wrong.

In 1938, my brother Lazaros was born and another year went by. My life in the village was peaceful. I worked hard, most of the time not knowing what the future held for me. Many times I would dream that one day I would be successful, but reality would come around and erase those fantastic dreams that I created in my world of fantasy. Poverty continued in our family.

It was in the summer of 1939 that Mr. Theofanis Tsirogianis who had twelve goats, one day said to my father, "Since Spiro doesn't have anything to do, I will give him the goats to take care of, and we will split the income from the milk for six years. At the end of six years, we will each take half of the new herd of goats." And that was how I became a shepherd overnight. Now, I had something to do. I kept the herd of goats in the mountains with the help of my cousin, Theodosi Kalampalikis, and my third cousin, Argiri Pournara. We spent our time under the pine trees and the clean crystal air. Life was beautiful! We were young, good kids who didn't drink or smoke.

It was 1940. The villagers had already started to cultivate the land. The snow was melting and the people began their excursions to Mouzaki and Arta bringing back news from the cities. There were no newspapers and televisions in the village. The mailman came once a week from the village Bragkiana and brought the mail and the news. We learned that Adolph Hitler in Germany was getting ready for war. The Prime Minister of Greece, Ioannis Metaxas, informed all the Greek people, especially the villagers, to cultivate all the parcels of their land even the gardens surrounding their houses, because hard times were ahead due to the impending war.

On October 28th 1940, at five o'clock in the afternoon the church bells suddenly started to toll in the village. The ringing continued, announcing that something terrible was happening. I was with my cousin Argiri in the mountains. We left the herd of goats and ran to the village to find out what was happening. We saw two soldiers who had came from Bragkiana Station to inform us that boys who were old enough, had to enlist in the army and were to present themselves to their divisions within twenty-four hours, because Italy was coming to invade Greece.

Mussolini sent a letter to the Italian ambassador in Athens informing the Prime Minister, Ioannis Metaxas, that the Duce was asking the authorization of the Greek government to permit the Italian army to occupy the island of Crete, the port of Piraeus, part of Epirus, and the north part of Greece, close to Albanian border. To this ultimatum, Ioannis Metaxas responded with only one historic word: Oxi (No). Thus, the Italian forces started the war with the main goal of trying to take over Greece. The invasion started from Albania where the Greek army was waiting for them.

In the village, conversation was all about the war. People reminisced about the atrocities they had to endure during the invasion of the Turks from 1912 to 1922, who had enslaved the Greeks for four hundred years. My grandmother was born in 1858. When she was growing up, she remembered the Turks in the village and narrated stories to me. Every time that the Turks would come to the village, it used to rain. Also, the Turks washed their hands before and after eating. In the village, we had a small fort called *Koulia from* where the villagers fought the Turks. My grandmother died in 1943 at the age of 82. I never knew my grandfather since he died at the age of 47. He was an alcoholic and my grandmother had to take care of their four children all alone. My grandfather had come from the village called Kamina, next to Empeso Baltou, and lived with my grandmother's family. His real name was Sklidas, but because he came often to the village to see my grandmother, he was given the nickname *Kalampalikis*. That is how we got the name *Kalampalikis*.

The war continued as we got ready for the winter. That year we had the worst winter in years with severe winds and cold. We could hear the cannons from afar as the Greek Army fought with the Italians at the border with Albania. News was limited in the village due to the broken telephone lines from the heavy snowfall. When the war started, the Balkan countries refused to trade with Greece making it more difficult for the Greek people. Greece had enough wheat and corn for only six months. The devastation brought on by hunger was already being felt in the big cities. The government was forced to ration bread in order to sustain its people. We were fortunate in our village. We still had a little bit of wheat and corn.

1941 was the year of starvation. Many didn't have anything to eat as we had depleted our store of wheat and corn. In my village, thirty-eight villagers died of hunger. The majority of them were elderly. Their hands, feet and eyes had become swollen from the hunger when they gave up their last breath of air. It was indeed sad to observe this tragic scene. We had come to the point of eating grass with just a little bit of meat to survive. At night, we couldn't sleep as the hunger kept us awake. We heard that the Greeks were winning the war, taking over the southern part of Albania and were advancing to the central capital. The winter passed and glimpses of spring appeared on the slopes of the villages. The chirping of the birds awakened the suffering and hungry villagers, whose only hope was to survive until the war was over. Spring was the season of abundance that year, the abundance of milk from the goats and sheep. It was enough to keep us going. I had lost a lot of weight and my legs became skinny from not having enough to eat. We had finished all the corn and had some meat left over to survive on.

It was a moment of devastation and lost hope. People were in the abyss of their existence. That was also true in our family. I remember my poor mother going without food so her hungry children could have food to eat. Many times the cupboards were empty. Nothing to eat! She looked around for a solution to keep her children alive. She didn't have a lot of possessions, except the sewing machine she used to make her children's clothes. It was her pride and joy as it was part of her dowry. One day, seeing her children starving, she took the drastic step to sell her only valuable household item, her *Singer sewing machine*. She received forty okathes of corn for her sewing machine which she sold to Mr. Kosfaki in the village called Soumerou.

At that time, due to starvation, there was a lot of thievery. People stole to survive. I was watching the goats and the best he-goat weighed almost thirty okathes. It was the most precious animal in my herd, and I was always afraid that they would steal him from me. One day, my cousin Stathoula Pournara and I had the herd by a mill called Fotis Nkolia. Suddenly, I heard Stathoula screaming that someone had taken the he-goat and he had a gun. I ran and I caught the he-goat by his hind legs and didn't let go. The thief turned towards me and hit me in the chest with the butt of the gun. He wore a hat, covering his eyes and his face. Due to our struggle, his hat fell off his head exposing his face to me. It was Ioannis Mpakatselos from the section of Akaila. Upon calling his name, he let go of the he-goat and ran off freeing the animal.

Everyone was waiting to find out what the end result of the war would be. Mussolini thought that within twenty-four hours he would have been the master of Greece, but he was not successful. On April 6, Adolph Hitler who although he had advised Mussolini that the Greeks were excellent fighters, had no other alternative but to invade Greece in order to save his friend Mussolini. Hitler sent six divisions to Greece entering from Macedonia. He conquered Greece in three days, breaking the Metaxa lines of the Greek Army without any difficulties. He entered Athens and from there Hitler's plan was to take over Turkey and finally conquer Russia. Athens was covered with swastikas especially on top of the Acropolis hill reminding the Greeks that they were under German control. In Crete, it took the German Army three months to take over the island. The Cretans fought like lions as Leonida did with the Spartans against the Persians.

We heard very little news about the war in the village. Some soldiers that had returned to the village brought back guns and their experiences from the battles. Two soldiers from our village were killed: Fotios Mparoutas and Chrisostomos Tsivolas.

The shortage of food continued. It was March and we still didn't have any food to eat. We were forced to eat acorns, grass and any other edible thing that we could find in the fields. Everyone was waiting for June, the reaping of the wheat. Hunger however, could not wait any longer and we cut the green wheat, roasted it, and made porridge. Our stomachs had shrunk from starvation and our esophagus were almost closed, making it difficult for us to swallow food. But we were lucky! All the spring, we milked the goats and sheep two times a day. That spring; we had so much milk that we milked them three times a day. The wheat fields were better than any other year and the fruit was in abundance. The villagers said that it was a *miracle!* The old men of the village said that such things never happened before. They stated that God felt sorry for the people of this small village.

The Germans never came to our village. There were no roads for them to use to get to the village, only herd paths were in existence. In the cities there were a lot of losses. When a German was killed, the Germans shot fifty Greeks. Also the people of the big cities suffered a lot from starvation. They waited hours in lines to receive a loaf of bread. The war continued without anyone knowing when it would be over. We heard the news that England and Russia were also fighting. In the village starvation was almost over. Wheat, grapes, figs and corn were in abundance in the autumn. We had something to eat, but still we took special care to make sure that we stored enough food for the next winter.

It was in the autumn of the same year that death came to visit our village. Two murders took place. Kostas Tolis, a seventy-five year old man, sold a piece of land to Theofani Tsirogiannis for a few pounds of corn, but later when he had eaten the corn, he changed his mind and wanted his land back. At that time, there were no documents for the sale of property. The son of Kostas Tolis, Filipos, went to the shop of Tsirogianni and started a fight on account of the property. Suddenly, Tsirogianni took out his pistol and fired, killing Filipos. Tsirogianni went to the parcel of land that he had bought from Kostas and built a hut in the center. I remember asking him what he was doing in that small hut and he said to me, "This is my land." Theofanis Tsirogiannis had a brother named Michalaki. One afternoon, not too long after the murder, Kostas Tolis went to visit his daughter-in-law. It was raining on that day. When he was returning from her house, Michalaki Tsirogiannis was waiting for him, and ended up slaughtering him with an ax. All the villagers were saddened by the incidents in the village. Of course this was all due to the war and the shortage of food.

I continued looking after the herd of goats with my cousins, regardless of the happenings in the village. Tsirogiannis had a large family: six boys and one girl called Iphigenia. Iphigenia used to come to the mountains to pick up the milk. She always has a smile on her face. Slowly, my love for her was increasing. She was twelve and I was fifteen years old. At that time, marriages took place with the help of a matchmaker. I had in mind to ask for her hand, but her father was very strict and so it remained only puppy love. One day, I had a fight and hit one of my friends, Basili Nanos, who was a shepherd for Dimitri Papathanasiou. He said that he would tell the brother of Iphigenia that she was my girlfriend. I told him that I just talked to the girl and nothing happened between the two of us. The next day, I was waiting for Iphigenia to come for the milk, but instead, I saw her mother coming towards me. She looked furious. I panicked! I didn't know what to do. I also felt sorry for Iphigenia. I was also fearful of her father, although I hadn't done anything wrong. A month went by and I decided to meet with her father and explain everything to him. One day, I saw him leaving the village with two mules headed for Prava. I caught up with him. My heart was beating quickly as if it wanted to explode. When I said good morning to him, he asked me how I was doing. I responded politely that everything was coming along fine and we kept on walking until we reached a small forest, where he pointed at a rock and told me to sit down. Suddenly, he took his gun out and told me to tell him the truth about his daughter. I told him that I hadn't touched his daughter, and that if he didn't believe me, he should take her to the doctor to see if she was still a virgin. I assured him that I was telling him the truth. After hearing me speak, he put his gun away and smiled. From that point on, I avoided both Iphigenia and him, ending my love for her. My meeting with Tsirogianis that day has been kept a big secret until now.

In the month of September, the rebels had gathered on the other side of Baltou in the high mountains of Gavrogos. We had no idea what it meant to be a rebel. At that time, Greece was an ally to England, who encouraged the Greeks in all the cities to fight the Germans. This brought more English troops to Greece to win the war.

It was another day in October. It started the same way as the previous ones, but this day turned out to be different when the villagers were summoned to the churchyard by the constant tolling of the church bell. Everyone from the fields, houses and those of us in the mountains came running to the churchyard to see what was happening. In front of the church, we saw about one hundred thirty men with guns and grenades dressed in army uniforms and some in civilian clothes. Among them was the General Napoleon Zervas who was giving a speech. He said that they came to the mountains in order to fight the Germans. Zervas was short and stuttered. He was born in Voulgareli in Epirus. He had gathered a good number of rebels to fight the Germans. A few men from our village joined him and were paid one gold coin for their efforts. At night, we could see fires in Gavrogos which was below our village, and later airplanes flew by dropping ammunition and food. The airplanes came from Corfu and Arta to Gavrogos, where Zervas had his base. They called Zervas' rebels, *nationalists*.

In 1943, Zervas' brother and two English lieutenants came to Argiri. They stayed for three months trying to connect to the periphery of Epirus and Evritanias. At that time the rebels had destroyed the bridge of Gorgopotamos in Lamia. In the month of December, Alekos Zervas and the two English lieutenants asked me to show them the way to Neo Argiri Evritanias. It took about two hours to show them the road. It was very cold. They were well dressed and rode their horses and I, on the other hand, was walking barefoot, and feeling and breaking the sharp ice with my feet. The English lieutenants told me that they would give me a pair of boots when the airplanes delivered supplies for the Greek Army. I thanked them for their kind words and when we reached the Neo Argiri, I left them. Meanwhile, I was waiting to see them again, anxious to receive my new boots, but they never returned to my village.

The rebels had taken over the mountains, the villages of Epirus, Thessali and Evritanias. The shortage of food continued in the village, but we didn't have anyone dying, as we had in the previous three years. In my family things were getting worse due to the fact that we were a large family and it was difficult to find enough food for everyone. I asked my father if I could go to the next village called Katafili to work for Lambro Fridas as a shepherd with sixty goats. In return he was going to pay me sixty okathes of wheat. That's what happened. My job as a shepherd started in the month of May. It was my first time leaving home. The three months passed by very quickly and when the time came for me to leave, Fridas looked sad and said this to me, "I am very happy with your work. I love you as my own son, and I hate to see you leave." I told him that I too had a great time working for him but I had to return to my village.

During the time that I was away, Argiri had changed a lot. Through Evritanias, the rebels came together to form an organization called EAM. When they came to the village they gave speeches and talked about communism. They emphasized that when they took over Greece, everyone would be equal. The rich would have to share their possessions with the poor.

The rebels started to have meetings in the village, singing communist songs, and shouting, "Long Live the KKE". I didn't go to the meetings in the village and neither did my brother Nicholas who was busy with his cobbler shop. I didn't like all the rebels meetings and I didn't believe what they were saying. I believed General Zervas and his army, the Nationalists. The army of EAM was called Amites. When the communist gathered on the outskirts of Thessali and Evritanias, Zervas withdrew from that area and returned to Valto and Tsimerka. At the same time the KKE took over EAM. They took away their property, called them nationalists, and many times, they killed them. In our village for example, Takis Tsiroginnis who was a retired policeman and had three hundred beehives was taken away. They hung him by the Avlakiou Bridge, but fortunately he lived. Then, they destroyed his property. I saw the disaster, terror and execution penetrating every corner of Greece.

My brother Nicholas in order to escape all the tortures of the rebels, left with my cousin Dimosthenis Pournara and went to Loutro, a village outside Amfilochia. The rebels didn't stay in one place. They spent two days in one village and the next day they went to a different one. When they came to our village, we had to supply them with bread, meat, cheese and other consumables. The people were becoming depressed, the war continued, and the communists were flourishing. The economy was ruined. The main concern for everyone was to save themselves.

In 1944 my mother at the age of 42 gave birth to my youngest brother Miltiadis. The communists had spread to every corner of Greece. Zervas was nowhere to be found, but when the communists and Zervas' division met, they fought viciously, slaughtering each other. It was a case of brother killing brother. In February an agreement was reached called the Agreement of Varkiza, which ordered the communists and nationalists to give up their rifles. This didn't last for too long. Again both sides picked up the rifles and were ready to fight.

One day my cousin Argiri Pournara and I decided to leave the village in order to visit our brothers in Loutro, to escape for a few days. It took us two days on foot to arrive in Loutro and we stayed for three days. On our return trip we carried with us twenty okathes of corn. The first night we reached the village Empeso surrounded by the big mountain called Kanala, it was getting dark and the cold from the severe winds penetrated our bodies right down to our bones. We had no water to drink, nowhere to stay and we were very tired. We decided to start a fire by the trunk of a tree and being so exhausted, we fell asleep. While we were sleeping the tree caught fire and fell down, almost killing us. The next day we arrived at another village called Vrouviana and the following day, we finally got back to our village, Argiri.

During our trip to Loutro, one more murder took place. Christos Papathanasiou, who for years was a rural guard in our village, began to threaten and insult the villagers who were KKE communists. The villagers had had enough of him, and one day caught him, beat him up and killed him with their shepherd's sticks. The accusers were Theodosios Papantonis, Ilia Mplanis and Ilia Tripogiorgos. Papathanasiou was thirty-three years old and had a brother Nick and sister

Fotini. There wasn't a day that went by that his mother couldn't be heard crying and shouting, "They killed my son! They killed my precious son! They killed my son!" She continued to cry and grieve for her son until she took her last breath of air. This was a very sad story in our village.

We heard very little news about the war, but what we heard was good news. We heard that the Germans were losing the war. Finally Germany lost the war in the spring of 1945. She started to withdraw her troops from Greece. When the Germans left, we thought that the war was over, but unfortunately one of the biggest disasters was just on the horizon, the Greek Civil War.

The snow had started to melt, bringing an end to another horrible winter. The communists were becoming more vicious than the Germans. They captured cities, took the supplies and whatever other items that they could carry with them. Greece, with the limited soldiers that she had, tried to protect the cities from the communists, but most of the time was unsuccessful. One of the cities that the communist took over was Karpenissi. They destroyed the whole city and depleted it of everything. In the villages, the communists constantly had trials against the nationalists and condemned the ones who had committed small crimes. The one in charge of these trials was Judge Katis. Communist fighting against the nationalists was escalating. The whole country was suffering without any true leaders to lead Greece to victory. The Communists killed many civilians, but many inhabitants from small northern villages in the mountains survived.

After the war, my family started to correspond with my uncle, my father's brother, who lived in the United States. We wrote letters to inform him of our condition. My uncle had left Greece in 1915. He arrived in Manchester New Hampshire and married Anastasia Kourtis.

My uncle and aunt Kalampalikis

In 1946, President Truman of the United States of America announced that they had to help Greece as it had suffered so much. We heard on the radio program, The Voice of America, that America was sending help through the organization called UNRRA (United Nations Relief and Rehabilitation Administration). The food supplies started to arrive in Greece in no time, after the President's announcement.

In the northern villages there was no transportation, neither did we have mules and horses, which meant that the only way to transport items was on our backs. It took us two days to go to Mouzaki to pick up the supplies, and two days to return to the village, carrying everything on our shoulders. The supplies that America sent to us were: flour, canned food, cheese and clothing. Every month, ten to fifteen villagers would leave the village headed for Mouzaki. In the evening we would stop and light a fire because it was very cold. We slept by the side paths. The first year, I went twenty times to Mouzaki, carrying twenty okathes of flour on my shoulders for my family. I had blisters on my shoulders and the rope would make deep cuts in my skin creating a river of blood. Not only did I carry supplies for my family, but also for the rebels we had to feed whenever they came to the village.

In September of 1946, we were informed that we had to go to Trikkala to receive a mule that our uncle had sent us from the United

States. He knew that we didn't have any animals to help us transport our supplies. There was a celebration, and much happiness in our family! We were going to have a mule! I went with my father to Trikkala and holding the number 310, we received our mule. My uncle had paid one hundred dollars for the mule. The mule was a lifesaver for all of us for the next five years, not only for our family, but also for the whole village. In 1951, however, the mule died of a sickness unknown to us. Everyone was saddened! We had lost our friend and a close member of the family.

Greece gathered more men in all the cities to fight the communists. In the village, New Argiri-Evritanias, five thousand rebels were present. We found out that their plan was to fight the Greek Army in Epirus. They called their fighters, comrades.

One day, when I had the herd in the section called Stefania, I saw an unknown figure coming towards Argiri. I was too far to see if he had a gun or not, but when he passed the mill of Kosta Ota, I heard a shot. He returned to the mill to ask for help from Theofani and Theodosi Ota. He told them that someone had shot him. They took good care of his wound and they took him back to Neo Argiri where the rebels were stationed. The next day the rebels came and surrounded the village, taking all the men to Neo Argiri, including my father. They interrogated them about the wounded rebel, and tortured them. The doctor finally figured out what had happened to the wounded rebel. He had wounded himself in order not to go to the battle. After three days, the men of our village returned home. I had seen the whole incident, but being fearful for my life, didn't say anything to anybody. I kept it a secret.

The rebels did not go to Epirus again. They went to Karpenissi. We heard that one of the ferocious communist captains, Aris Velouchiotis, was staying in the village of Velouxi, outside Karpenissi. He had thirty men with horses, all of them wearing black hats, which gave them their nickname, "mavroskoufithes".

The UNRRA continued supplying us with food. One day, thirty of our villagers went to Mouzaki. In the evening due to a delay, we had to stay in Mouzaki instead of returning home. We went to sleep in a place where they served meals. As we lay on the floor, we kept counting the hours till our return home. Around midnight, we heard shots and cannons being fired. Two thousand rebels were attacking Mouzaki. The Greek Army was not present in Mouzaki. It only had the police and a few guards. The rebels had come from Monastriri outside Mauromati. In the end, the rebels were unable to succeed and withdrew from Mouzaki. At nine o'clock in the morning, they told us that we could leave. When leaving the inn where we had slept, we saw three dead rebels on a carriage being taken to the cemetery. We left and thanked God for being alive. We told the people of our village what had happened to us in Mouzaki. The terror was escalating! In March 1947, two thousand rebels came to Argiri. We didn't know what was happening. Around eight o'clock in the evening, we heard a knock at our door and we saw our first cousin Xenophon Kalampalikis, an armed rebel. He told me that I had to enlist for the cause. I couldn't say anything. We started our journey, taking with us Charis Tripogiorgos and headed toward Kedra-Euritanias. When we reached the first two houses, the rebel told me to knock at the door to enlist another man that we needed. I went and knocked at the door of Nasios Mplani, but his wife told me that he wasn't in. Then, I knocked at another door. Ioannis Mplanis opened the door and I told him that we needed another comrade. He asked me where we were going and I told him that I didn't know, because the rebels never told us our destination and what we were going to do. Finally, we passed the village Kedra and reached the village Kerasies where someone by the name Zacharakis lived and had a mule. On the mule, we placed the two large land mines and some other equipment and came back to Argiri. I kept wondering what they were going to do with the land mines. By daylight we had reached a place called Skripta. On the other side, we could see the Avlaki Bridge. In the morning, we saw and heard the mortars very close to us. Finally we understood what the rebels' plan was: They wanted to destroy the Avlaki Bridge with the land mines.

The Avlaki Bridge

The river Acheloos flows under the Avlaki Bridge dividing Evritanias, Thessali and Epirus. The river was dangerous to cross, especially in the winter and spring when the snow melted. Before they built the bridge, the villagers used to cross the river by holding on to a heavy rope that had been secured from one side to the other. The construction of the bridge began in 1908 by Italian engineers and personnel and was finished in 1912.

We were waiting for the order to continue towards the bridge. We were fearful as we heard loud and constant mortar explosions. The captain, who was in charge of us and the mission, was called Ypsilandis. He was a nervous and vicious person who always insulted us. Around ten o'clock, he received the order to continue and asked us if we knew the way to the bridge, but nobody spoke up. He was angry at our behavior and like a beast picked up his shepherd's stick and since I was closest to him, hit me on my back. Then, seeing how furious he was when he took his pistol out from its case, I spoke up and told him that I knew the path to the bridge. We started on our journey to the bridge when suddenly a rebel came to meet us. He wanted to talk to Ypsilandis. Ypsilandis told us to wait until his return. Then, he disappeared in the small forest to have his conversation with the other rebel. Being curious,

I followed him using another path, in order to find out what the conversation was all about. As I hid unnoticed behind some bushes in the forest, I heard the rebel saying to Ypsilantis that we couldn't go to the bridge, because it had already been taken over by the National Army. I was happy with the good news and ran back to the group to tell them that the Greek Army was close; and they had taken over the bridge. Ypsilandis returned to the group upset and mad. He didn't talk to us until we arrived at the huts of Kosera where he told us to leave the mines and equipment and return to our village. I took the path to my village, and when I arrived home, I told my mother that I had to hide in a place called Kalamakia for three days until I was sure that the rebels had left the village.

Three days went by and Theofanis Tsirogiannis was getting ready to go to Arta for shopping. I thought that the Greek Army would come to the village, and without any fear, I went with Tsirogiannis to Arta. He asked me why I was going to Arta with him and I said that I had to sell a goat for corn. My parents backed me up and told me that it was a good idea to be absent for a few days from the village. When we arrived at the bridge, the Greek Army was there. We were so lucky that the rebels didn't destroy the bridge. Finally we arrived in Arta. I sold the goat, took twenty okathes of corn on my shoulders and returned to the village.

While I was gone for five days from the village, the famous Karampinas from Klidi, Artas, crossed the Avlaki Bridge and came to Argiri with his division of fifty men, who were all nationalists. They were fighting against the communists. We always had the problem of intruders in the village. One day it was the Nationalists and the next day the Communists. Each one of them had their own stories of sufferings to narrate. Karampinas was very strict. When he came to Argiri, he right away asked for the men who went to blow up the Bridge of Avlaki. They found Ioannis Mplani and interrogated him. He told them the truth that the communists forced us to go with them, but we never reached the bridge because the Greek Army was there. Karampinas was furious, and insulted the men of Argiri and he shot Mplani with his gun.

Ioannis Mplani had fought against the Turks in 1922. He was captured but escaped. Now, after so many years, it was unfortunate to be killed by a Greek, the vicious Karampinas.

Karampinas also had my name and searched for me, but I was nowhere to be found. I was very lucky. Karampinas then went to the village Kedra-Evritanias and after two days, he returned to Epirus. I didn't have a clue about what was happening in the village, and when I returned from Arta, my mother embraced me with tears in her eyes. She told how lucky I was that I wasn't in the village. I would have met the same end as Mplani.

Things were getting worse. In August 1947, the communists came again to the village. This time they saw the mule that our uncle had sent us, and before we had the time to hide it, they took it away. The thief was Kiritsis from the village of Karditsa. My father took some walnuts and a bottle of our potent liquor called *tsipouro* and went to see Lieutenant Kiritsis to beg him for the return of our mule, as it was so vital for our family. The Lieutenant promised him that they would return the mule. Our mule was fearful of strangers. None of the communists were able to place the saddle and the halter on the mule. The only person that the mule was comfortable with was me. For a month, Kiritsis tried to tame the mule, but he was unsuccessful. Thus, he gave the order for the mule to be returned to the Kalampalikis. No sooner did he give the order that the mule was returned to our village. I was so happy! I put the halter and the saddle on his back without any problem.

In the village of Prasia-Evriatanias, two hours away from my village, the president Christos Ntasiotis had two mules that often went to Amfilochia to receive supplies from UNRRA for his people. When he arrived at the village of Sikaretsi with the supplies, the communists caught him and interrogated him. He told them that he was a communist like they were, but they didn't believe him and accused him of being a nationalist. They took away his mules and the supplies and killed him, leaving behind his two sons and a daughter by the name of Georgia, whom my brother Nicholas later married.

The people from the villages of Evritanias, Neo Argiri, and Topolina started to leave for the village of Kompoti, outside Arta. On September 15, 1947, my brother Nicholas and I told our parents that we too were going to Kompoti. We took the mule, my brother's cobbler tools, and one blanket and left the village. We only had the clothes on our backs. On my feet I wore a pair of shoes that had wooden soles. When I walked one could hear my steps from far away. That was all we had. We did not have any money.

Our journey to Kompoti began. On the first night, we stayed at the house of a very nice family in the village called Kerasia. On the second day we reached Kompoti around five o'clock in the afternoon. Outside the church, we saw many villagers, around two hundred of them. They were refugees from the villages of Neo Argiri and Topolina.

Kompoti had 2,000 inhabitants and was half an hour away from Arta. The people were very kind and hospitable. They too were refugees from Asia Minor and felt our pain. They were famous for growing the best oranges in Greece. Kompoti is also the birthplace of Nicholas Skoufas, the founder of the organization called *Filiki Etairia*.

Kompoti

In Kompoti we found a relative, Fotis Koultoukis, who stayed at the house of Spiros Kouloulis who gave us a room to stay in without paying rent. My brother Nicholas began to carry out his trade as a cobbler, fixing the shoes of the refugees. He had a lot of work but received very little money. I didn't have anything to do and I joined Mr. Kouloulis gathering wood for fire. We had a severe, cold, winter. We didn't have a lot of snow, but since were close to the river Platania, the severe winds never ceased to blow. I was also busy taking care of the mule.

Uncle Costa with Aunt Elene Kalampalikis and Aunt Sophia Tsiamis

In the winter, we didn't receive any news from our village, from our parents, our three brothers and our sister Konstantia. I saw that the kids in Kompoti were well dressed and I was saddened at not being able to be like them. I always thanked God for being alive after all the suffering that I had gone through.

In 1948, the Greek government built tin huts for the refugees. UNRRA also continued supplying us with food and clothes. I was lucky to receive a long coat. Our worry was that the communists often ambushed us on our way back to Kompoti and stole our supplies, clothes, and our animals.

On July 20th 1948, Fotis Koultoukis and I took the mules and went to Arta to load flour that UNRRA was giving to the refugees of Kompoti .When we arrived we tied the mules at the inn of Vasilis Chouliara and went to the storage area where they distributed the supplies. When we returned, the mules were gone. We asked the owner,

Vasilis Chouliara, where our mules went and he said that the Greek soldiers had taken them away. We went to the barracks and there they were our mules tied to a tree. When we met with the captain, we told him that the mules were ours. He replied that the Greek Army was using the mules, and if we wanted to go with them, he would pay us. I told him that I would never leave my mule alone since it was a special gift from my uncle from the United States. Thus, I took up his offer. Koultoukis decided not to come along with us.

It took us two hours to load the mules with the ammunition and we left for the village Peta. It was a very hot day in July. We passed Peta and were headed for Kaliantini. We had no idea of our final destination. The only thing that we knew was clear was that we were with the Greek soldiers and not with the barbaric communists. When we arrived on the outskirts of Kaliantini, we camped on one of the high hills for that night. We didn't have any water from five o'clock in the afternoon until ten o'clock the next morning. The next day, since we were all suffering from thirst, I was unable to swallow anything. As we were walking down the narrow paths, we found a small stream. Everyone ran to drink the water, but the captain shouted, "Do not to drink the water! It is contaminated!"

The second day was July 21, and as we walked to Tzoumerka, we came upon a Greek army of 400 soldiers. At five o'clock in the afternoon, we had reached the village Voulgareli, the birth place of General Napoleon Zervas. It was a beautiful village with well-built houses, but it was uninhabited on account of the communists. We camped on the mountains above the village. For me this experience was just like a vacation. I had food, company, and was safe. My family however didn't know where I was. They only knew that I was with the Greek soldiers and not with the communists. Thus, they didn't worry too much.

I belonged to the first platoon, and had two mules to carry ammunition. The soldiers told me to dig a trench in case the communists attacked us. I dug a very deep trench and surrounded it with stones. One civilian with a lot of experience told me that there was no need to dig a trench because the rebels were scared to attack us. But suddenly, to our surprise, the rebels attacked us in the morning. We heard

31

the cannons and the bullets flying over our heads. My friend, jumped into the trench as fast as he could, but a large stone fell on his head. He was wounded and in no time, his face was covered with blood. The battle went on until ten o'clock, when the rebels decided to leave. They headed north. We had one wounded soldier and two mules were killed. After forty days, the soldiers received the order to return to Arta. They gave me the mules and two hundred drachmas. I was really happy I had served my country.

I came back to Kompoti where my brother Nicholas lived. For me, the most important thing was to find out how my family was doing in the village. We heard that the rebels were recruiting the civilians and forcing them to fight against the Greek Army. The news was devastating. I told my brother that I had to get my sister Konstantia, who was sixteen years old, away from the village and bring her to Kompoti. He gave me his blessing and told me to be careful with the rebels.

My journey from Kompoti was long. I stayed the first night in the village of Kerasia just below the mountain of Gavrogos. The second night, I was really worried because passing through Gavrogos was very dangerous. There were a lot of rebels hiding in the mountains, which meant that there was a possibility of being recruited by them. I crossed myself and continued on my journey. When I arrived in Goupata, I met with Trimpos from the village Skoulikaria, who was insane. He told me stories about when the Germans came to his village. He said that all the villagers had left Skoulikaria and were living in the forest. They didn't want to be captured by the Germans. Trimpos had a one-year-old son and was constantly crying from hunger. In order to solve the problem of his crying, and so as not to be discovered by the Germans, he took the child and hit him against a tree trunk until the child died. After telling his stories, he asked me where I was going. I told him that I was going to get my sister from the village because I didn't want the rebels to take her with them. He called me a communist over and over again. I told him that I was not a communist. I also told him that I stayed in Kompoti and spent forty days with the Greek National Army in Voulgareli. He became sane again and calmed down. I continued moving ahead toward the large area where the rebels were hiding.

It was the month of October. Silence prevailed around me and the breeze was bathing my tormented body. Only the chirping of the birds could be heard. My heart was beating fast as I was approached the large area where the rebels were often stationed. I walked in fear waiting to hear, "Alt" (stop). I was lucky! There were no rebels hiding in the forest that day. From afar, I saw the chapel of St. Ilia above our village. I made the sign of the cross and thanked God for my safety, the safety of my village, and my family.

Upon seeing my sister, I told her that very early the next morning, we were leaving for Kompoti. That night we heard that the rebels had entered the village of Raftopoulo-Evritanias, four hours by foot from our village. The next day, my sister and I began our trip to Kompoti. As we were passing through New Argiri and were headed for the Avlaki Bridge, we met with the two daughters of Stelios Kalinkou who were also going to Kompoti.

In Raftopoulo, Argiris Pournaras and Nicholas Mpourdouvalis were gathering chestnuts. The rebels caught them and asked them the names of all the men and women aged between seventeen and fifty, living in Argiri. The following day, the rebels took over our village. They took the daughter of my uncle Kostas and one of his sons. My uncle begged them not to take his daughter. He was willing to give them another son if they allowed his daughter to stay behind. At the beginning, the rebels agreed but later took the daughter and the two sons with them into the mountains. This abduction of children called "Paidomazoma" happened very often in the northern villages of Argithea and Evritanias.

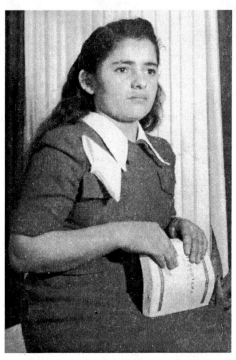

Spiros' first cousin, Aphrodite Kalampalikis. She ended up in Poland during the abduction of children: **The Paidomazoma**

I was of age to join the Greek National Army, but when we looked at the army's registration list, my name could not be found. When I was born in 1927, my parents didn't bother to register me in the village. If I didn't take the initiative to enlist, I would have been incarcerated for two years. I immediately went to Nomarchia Karditsis.

At that time, Kostas Tsiakalos from the village Katafili was going to Trikala and I joined him. We left by bus from Kompoti and arrived in Metsovo on our first night. Metsovo is a beautiful town and also the birthplace of Averof. In the morning, we waited a long time for the bus. It had a hard time passing the highest peak called Katara, due to thick fog. It was ten o'clock before the sky cleared and we were able to continue on our trip. We reached Katara where the Greek Army's guards were stationed. They stopped the bus, checked our papers and told the driver that there were two soldiers who were returning to their houses and they wanted him to take them to Trikala. The bus driver refused and told them that the bus was private and he couldn't fulfill their wish. He left them behind, following his daily schedule. The two guards found another bus and gave the order to follow the first bus so the could take care the bus driver. The buses reached the peak of Katara one after the other. When the two guards alighted from the bus, they ordered the driver of the first bus to get off the bus, which he did. They beat him up and told him to continue on his trip to Trikala, taking them along, if he wanted to be alive. And that was what happened. The two guards joined us on the trip to Trikala. Tsiakalos lived in Trikala and got off the bus. I continued to Karditsa where my cousin Athena Pournara lived. In no time, I found an attorney, Ilia Zioga, a relative of my mother, who prepared my papers. Then, I went to the prefecture where I met with five officials. They took care of all of my papers. Finally, I returned to Metsovo, Ioannina, and back to Kompoti.

Another winter went by. By this time, my parents and my three brothers had suffered a lot in the village. The lack of communication had isolated them from the rest of the world. The Greek Army was stationed in Avlaki-Baltou. The rebels had taken over Argithea, Evritanias, recruiting everyone to fight the National Greek Army. They also used elderly people like my mother, who was fifty years old, to carry supplies and to perform other duties.

Finally spring arrived. The year was 1949. For the first time, I found a job in Kompoti. My bosses were George Fakos and Ilias Poulizos who were the owners of many orange groves. With horses, we plowed the vast orchards, planting corn and wheat. For payment, they gave me wheat and corn since money was hard to come by. For me, it was great, since I finally had something to do. The summer passed without me knowing if my own family was still alive.

It was at this time that Greece became an ally of Great Britain. Seeing that the rebels had taken over almost three quarters of Greek territory, Prime Minister Churchill asked the United States to help Greece before it became a communist country. The United States intervened, making Papagos the head of the Greek National Army. Under the banner of the United States and the powerful command of Papagos, they began to defeat the communists and pushed them behind the Iron Curtain.

George Fakos: Spiro worked for him for one year

In the summer of 1949, without any warning, the villages became the target for the rebels. The people were suffering. The forceful recruitment and the brutal killings continued. The Greek Army seeing that the people were suffering, gave the order to leave the villages. They gave them only a few hours to gather their belongings and their animals and to head for the Avlaki Bridge where the National Army was stationed, protecting the villagers from the rebels. In our village only two elderly people, Apostolis Ottas, ninety years old, and Georgia Tsivolas, ninety-one years stayed behind. They put them in one house in the village and gave them enough supplies to survive on. The soldiers told them not to give any information to the rebels if they came to the village. Then, after much thinking, one of the captains gave the order to kill them. He was fearful that they would tell the rebels the truth. And so, two more innocent lives were lost to the powerful bullets of the rifle. The atrocities and executions continued. The following people lost their lives during the Civil War: Theofanis Kalampalikis, Theodosios Kalampalikis, Argiris Pournaras, Martha

Pournaras, Nikolas Mparoutas, Basiliki Mparouta Dimitrios Mplanis, George Tripogiorgos, Panteli Zverdas, and the two sergeants and one police officer: Grigoris Papantonis, Pavlos Zaharakis, Lazarus Tsivolas and Lamros Papantonis. All were killed fighting against the communist rebels.

After a few days, I heard that my parents and siblings were alive and were coming to Kompoti. When I saw them after so many months of separation, I didn't recognize them. They were dressed in rags and with them were ten goats, the animals that the rebels had forgotten in the huts. The refugees increased in number. They were coming in large numbers from the villages of Arta, Amfilochia and Agrinion.

The winter had engulfed the whole territory of Kompoti, making the refugees very cold. The cold and suffering of the people never ceased to exist. Their only hope was for the quick arrival of spring when the Greek Army was going to start to fight the rebels again, from the south to the north until every one of them was out of Greece.

In March of 1950, the artillery and infantry of the Greek Army came to Kompoti. They knew ahead of time that ten thousand rebels were coming to attack Kompoti and Arta. They were coming from Gavrogos passing through the village Dimargio and finally to the outskirts of Kompoti where our soldiers were waiting for them. It was my first time seeing three rebels entering Kompoti to face the Greek Army. With them, there were other civilians that the rebels had recruited forcefully from the mountains. The battle lasted for two days and the rebels were unable to take over Kompoti. Disappointed, the rebels took refuge in the mountains. They dispersed to the surrounding villages of Aponopetrous, Kaliantini and Tzoumerka. This was the last battle of the KKE rebels. From the central part of Greece, they gathered in the highest mountains of Macedonia called the Mountains of Grammos and Vitsi until the Greek Army pushed them behind the Iron Curtain. Those that the rebels had recruited in 1948, along with the top officials ended up in Poland and Hungary. I hope and pray that this kind of catastrophe will never take place again.

It was May 1950. Finally, the Greek people felt the air of liberation. The Greek army gave the order for the refugees of Argithea and

Evritanias to return to their villages. It had been ten years of wars, first with the Italians, then the Germans and then the Civil War. It was a life of misery, execution, terrorism and tyranny. With the spirit of being free again, we gathered our limited belongings, and headed for our villages. We were fearful of the conditions that we were going to find in Argiri after the Civil War. It took us two days to arrive in our village. There was hardly anyone there. It was empty. The birds too, had disappeared along with the dogs and cats that had died of starvation. The grass was five feet tall, a true jungle among the beauty of Nature.

With courage, we began to cultivate the land and to reconstruct our houses. Life was slowly returning to a normal pace as before. UNRRA still continued to supply us with food and clothing. They even gave us mules to transport supplies from the big city to the village and at the same time to cultivate the land. My brother Nicholas opened up a café in the village, and also continued his trade as a cobbler. I was working in the fields and transporting supplies for the villagers.

At that time my aunt and uncle from the United States wrote a letter to my father asking him to send one of his six children to America. They didn't have any children. My father agreed. It was decided that my brother Tom, age thirteen would be the one to go. We sent Tom's documents to my uncle, and within two months the invitation and legal papers arrived for his trip to the United States.

Tom Kalampalikis in America with my uncle George and aunt
Anastasia and Anna Mermingis

I took my brother Tom to Athens. Good thing we had our aunt
and uncle Ioannis Kartali living in Athens. We stayed in their house.
We went to the embassy where we had to wait for many hours and
days, due to the large crowd also waiting for their papers. Due to the
lack of money, and having to wait for days to receive the proper docu-
mentation for Tom, I decided to return to the village. Tom stayed behind and with the help of my uncle he was able to go to the embassy,
when it was necessary. Three months went by until finally Tom had all
the papers and his visa ready for the United States. We wrote a letter
to my uncle including pictures of Tom, informing him that Tom was
ready for his trip to the United States. Tom departed from Athens on
July 21, on a ship called La Guardia. It took him twelve days to arrive in America where my aunt and uncle were waiting anxiously to
see their first relative since they left Greece in 1915. The only way we
communicated with my uncle was by letter since there were no tele-
phones in the village.

When I returned to the village from Athens, I heard the devastating news that my beloved animal and friend, the mule that my uncle
had sent us from America, had died. I was not the only one affected by
this great loss, the whole village mourned for our mule. The mule was

the only means of transporting supplies from the cities to the village for all the villagers. After this incident, my brother Nicholas bought two mules for me to go to Mouzaki. I spent five days in Mouzaki and Arta loading flour and other items for our village. During one of my excursions to Arta, I encountered a large group of people gathered in the main square of the town. I looked around to see what was happening and to my amazement, I saw the famous Karampinas, the one who had shot the innocent Ioannis Mplani in my village. Karampinas had a small monkey on his shoulder. Suddenly, a civilian approached him and started to hit him on his head with his shepherd's stick. Blood covered his whole face. Good thing the police came and he was saved, otherwise he could have been killed. I said then to myself, "You get what you deserve!"

On January 2, 1952, a notice came for me to enlist in the army and I had to present myself in the city of Theva, to the infantry division. When I left the village, all the mountains were covered with snow and it was very cold. I had to walk against the vicious winds until finally I arrived in Theva. I became part of the infantry division and our training consisted of severe military exercises. They beat us daily with belts and shouted: "Run faster you lopsided Johns, run faster!" These kind of military exercises were called "kapsonia". We lost appetite due to exhaustion. We hardly ate anything for two weeks. Some of my friends became depressed and cried. As a matter of fact, one of them wanted to commit suicide. I, on the other hand who had suffered a lot in life, wasn't afraid of anything. My lieutenant was from Lamia and the rebels had killed his brother. He became insane. Another colleague of mine didn't want to carry a rifle, which meant extra exercises and beatings for the rest of us until he accepted to carry it. Every day, we were busy with daily exercises and target practice.

One day we went to practice with hand grenades. There were two hundred soldiers. The lieutenant asked for someone to be the first one to use a grenade. I was more than willing to oblige. Then the lieutenant told me that I had to throw the grenade thirty yards and try not to kill anyone. I had no problem doing this which satisfied the lieutenant. I was proud to be the first one to participate in any kind of military exercise because the army was like schooling to me, and I was proud to wear the Greek uniform with the crown on my soldier's cap.

Spiros in Greek Army Uniform

After three months, I was transferred to another division in Neapoli- Kozani where the military exercises were much more extensive. We had two batteries and four hundred soldiers doing target practice and running at the same time. I was the second best in the four hundred yards. I stayed for fifteen months in Neapoli. At that time, the artillery had abolished mountain climbing and I was ordered to be part of the plat plain artillery of Pavlou Mela in Thessalonica. The plain artillery was new for me. I was to become a marksman. The exercises with the missiles were a big success.

My mother had a sister in Thessalonica married to Tsiatsou who had three sons and a daughter. It was my first time meeting them, and I visited them whenever I had free time.

The time was approaching for my release from the army. I became a civilian in July 1954, after twenty-nine months in the service. I asked my cousins to find me a job in Thessalonica, but there were no jobs. This was due to the Civil War. The country was depleted of its resources and the economy was in a devastating condition. While I lived in Thessalonica, I will never forget the severe cold winds that engulfed the city, called *Bardaris*.

They told me that many people died from those severe winds especially when the Germans recruited soldiers from Africa and brought them to Thessalonica. They were unable to withstand the cold weather and within a few days they found them dead and frozen.

I left Thessalonica by train for Karditsa. I was thinking about on what I was going to do in the village. There was no future for me there. It was at that time that I wrote a letter to my uncle asking him if I could join him in the United States. When I arrived at my village everyone was after me to get married. There was a girl the same age as myself, who offered me fifty gold coins to get married to her. I told her family that I had no interest in getting married and I was getting ready to go to the United States.

Uncle George and Aunt Anastasia

I wrote another letter to my uncle and aunt to send me the legal invitation to come as a refugee to the United States. They agreed. For months, I waited anxiously for the invitation. From June 1954, it arrived in November 1955 from the American Embassy. To come to the

United States, one had to be cleared of any participation in the communist organizations, which existed during the Civil War. A crew from the Embassy came to Karditsa to talk to the people to make sure that I was never involved in the communist party. They met with a friend of the family, Basilis Kotsiori, from the village Bragkiana. He gave them the best recommendation and said that I was never involved with the KKE communist party and was a nationalist who served in the Greek Army. Then, the crew left for Athens.

In a few days, I received a letter from the American Embassy to come to Athens. My mother was saddened about my decision to leave for the United States, but deep down she knew that my life would be better and I would be able to help the family economically. The autumn of 1956 was over when I left for Athens. I went to the American Embassy for my papers and had a physical examination. Everything was coming along fine. On March 14, 1956 I received the visa. It was one of the happiest days of my life. I bought my ticket for the United States with the ship Olympia, and I left for America on the first of April.

I had two weeks free until my departure. I couldn't leave without saying good-bye to my parents and therefore I returned to Mouzaki. Argithea was covered in snow. I walked for many hours and I found some other people to keep me company, passing the village of Oxia. The snow was so high that one couldn't see the beech-trees. Only the peaks of the trees could be seen. I said good-bye to the whole village, and my mind was full of thoughts of my trip to America. I found it very difficult saying goodbye to my parents. My father blessed me and wished me a nice trip and asked me to say hello to his brother George and his wife Anastasia. He also stressed that I had to write to them often. My mother accompanied me to the outskirts, two kilometers away from the village, not wanting to let go of me. I promised her that I would return soon and not to worry about me. Embracing her, I felt her tender motherly love for me as I noticed the uncontrollable tears running down her cheeks. Looking at her for the last time, I left for Athens.

In Athens, my uncle John and my aunt Vasiliki Kartalis had a daughter Effie who had helped my brother Tom and now helped me to get all the papers in order for my departure. I immediately wrote my uncle a letter that my day of departure was the first of April on the ship Olympia. I was very fortunate to travel with my first cousin Dimitris Tiligada and two boys from Koumpouriana, called Pozios. I met them in Pireus.

The time finally came for my departure. Upon boarding the big ship, I crossed myself and thanked God for being alive and in good health after going through such difficult times during the wars. I said to myself, "Spiro your new life is unfolding in front of you." I was twenty-nine years old.

The ship was luxurious and it had 1200 passengers not including the crew. It had a chapel, theater, and whatever else was needed. The food was excellent and for me it was a true paradise. We reached Italy and stayed there for four hours, picking up more passengers for America. The second stop was in Lisbon, Portugal. We had the opportunity to disembark and visit the capital where I bought a ring for two dollars. It looked gold and had a stone like a diamond. Of course, since I paid two dollars, it couldn't have been a gold ring, but for me it was a novelty. From Lisbon, we entered the vast Atlantic Ocean, counting the days until our arrival at our destination. One day the sea was rough. I saw the tables tumbling over, dishes breaking, and food was scattered everywhere. I became sea sick. The next stop was in Halifax, Canada. As we approached the port, we saw a white scene of snow and felt the cold wind when we stepped outside. The mast of the ship was covered with ice. The days were getting shorter and shorter now until our arrival in New York. My excitement was increasing daily as I looked forward to our arrival in the United States. I was curious to see the way the Americans lived, to hear their language and to observe their customs.

The last night of our trip, there was a big gala dance to thank the captain for a safe trip. They were organizing the program for that night and were asking for participants who could dance different dances. My cousin and I wrote down our names to dance tsamiko. When the time came for us to enter the dancing hall, they demanded that we wear a tie. Before I left from Athens, I asked my uncle Yianni to teach me how to tie a tie, which I practiced during my trip. It kept me occupied. I didn't have a problem wearing a tie but my cousin didn't have a tie and was not allowed to enter the dancing hall. We had to come up with a solution since he was part of our dancing group. Finally, we thought of a clever way to distract the hostess by the door. My friend and I would talk to the lady by the door as my cousin slipped in through the door without being seen. And that is how we got him into the hall. Our trick worked perfectly. We had a marvelous time that evening.

The next day when we disembarked at the port of New York we passed by the beautiful "Statue of Liberty". It was on April 12, 1956 when I stepped foot on American soil, on Ellis Island, with only eight dollars in my pocket. I looked around! There were policemen everywhere. A hot dog peddler was selling hot dogs. Being curious as to what is was, I bought one along with an American cup of coffee. I took a sip of the coffee and I found it to be horrible, so I threw it away. I asked a policeman where the men's room was. With a smile, he led me to the men's room.

On the ship I was fortunate to meet a lady by the name Olga Skilogiani who was also going to Manchester New Hampshire. She told me that she was waiting for her brother to pick her up. I told her that I too, was going to Manchester New Hampshire and I didn't know if my uncle was coming to pick me up and asked if it was possible to travel with them. She had no objection. I went to look for my luggage, which was placed in the storage area, alphabetically. Before I got to the storage area, I heard someone calling my name. I thought that was my uncle, but from the pictures that he had sent to us in Greece, the man didn't look like him. The man with the beard who was calling my name was a stranger. As I approached him to find out his identity, he told me that he was a friend of my uncle, and my uncle had asked him to pick me up when he picked up his sister Olga.

On the way to Manchester, New Hampshire, we encountered much snow and very cold weather. It was night time when we arrived in Manchester where my uncle and aunt were waiting for me. My brother Tom who was attending high school then, and working at night, was not home yet. When he returned home later on, I told him all the news from the village.

After two days, I went out with my brother Tom to get acquainted with the City of Manchester. When he left Greece he was thirteen years old and now he was eighteen, spoke fluent English, and looked like a true American. When he showed me the city which was covered with snow, and the roads were filthy with the sand used to melt the snow, I wasn't very enthused. Perhaps, I was tired from my trip and the anxiety of finding a job, made me feel uncomfortable since I did not know a word of English. That was not a problem however, since there were many Greeks who lived in Manchester and one could hear the Greek language everywhere.

One week passed, and I asked Tom to help me find a job. At that time, there were a lot of mills and shoe shops in Manchester. I found a job at the Waumbec Mills. I started my job after being in America for ten days. The first day, my brother Tom went with me up to the entrance door of the Mill. I asked him, "What should I say to them if they say something to me in English?" My brother Tom told me to say, "I don't speak English." That was the only sentence that I used until I became comfortable with the English language. I began work in a large room which had four hundred automatic looms. The noise was deafening in the room with all the windows closed. I worked the second shift, from three o'clock in the afternoon until eleven o'clock at night. They paid me one dollar and sixteen cents per hour. My work was to cut the fabric from the looms, and to put it in the carriage, and that is why they called me the carriage boy. My boss's name was Louie. There were other Greeks in the mill and that made it easier for me when I needed an interpreter. At the beginning, I thought that since I didn't speak the English language everyone would look and laugh at me, but the opposite happened. Whenever I went to the mill or to the bank, people were willing to help me. That impressed me the most. That is why I love the United States. No other country can catch up with the service for others, the education, helping people in general and the progress that we have in the United States. I will never forget the help that the United States gave to Greece during the years of 1945-1952.

Tom, Spiros and Uncle George

In 1956 when I came to America, to my dismay I found out that life was not that expensive. Coffee was ten cents, a drink thirty five cents and postage stamps five cents. In the mills where I worked, sixty percent of the people were Polish. They were very good people and excellent workers.

Every time that I got paid, I always went to the bank and got a check to send to Greece. In 1951, we had bought some land in the village for about one thousand dollars. My uncle from America had sent us five hundred dollars and we still owed five hundred dollars, which we had to pay as soon as possible.

When I finished my job at eleven o'clock at night my boss always asked me if I could work four hours overtime. Thus, I worked until three o'clock in the morning. My boss communicated with me by showing me his four fingers, which meant four extra hours. Within one year I was able to pay off the five hundred dollars for the land in the village, and I still continued to send money to help my parents and my siblings.

Theo John and Thea Vasiliki Kartalis

After a year at the same job, I was promoted to weaver. It was a very nice lady by the name Clara from Poland who taught me how to do this job. They gave me thirty looms and pretty soon I had forty looms to work with. My hourly pay went up from one dollar and sixteen cents to one dollar seventy cents. I learned this job very well and without any difficulty. They gave me a design and I had to make it wearing white gloves, so as not to dirty the cloth. My big boss would visit me and always say to me, "Very good job, Spiro!" He was very satisfied with my work.

My life was very restricted. I stayed in the house of my uncle without paying any rent. My aunt was a wonderful lady and especially good at cooking. Whatever money I had left over, I would buy clothes, shoes and anything else that I needed. My English language was not improving much. However, when I went to the bank, I always went to the same teller because he understood my limited vocabulary. One day he said, "You send all of your money to Greece. What is going to happen to you when you get sick and are out of work?" I understood what he said to me but I couldn't respond to him. I didn't have the time to go to night school to learn the English language, because I slept during the daytime and worked at night. I loved watching television especially the Indian movies but I was frustrated I couldn't understand what was being said. In the neighborhood where I lived with my uncle, there was a sixteen year old girl who always told me that I was handsome, but I didn't understand her and I asked my aunt to translate for me. Generally, it is very hard when one doesn't speak the language.

As the time went by, my life was getting better. On the weekends, I usually went to the Greek dances with my friends. My brother Nicholas continuously wrote to me asking for money. Whenever I received his letters, I was disturbed and many times I couldn't sleep. I wrote to him that my job was very hard and unhealthy and when I got off from my work, I was covered in white cotton.

My youngest brother Miltiadis had just finished grammar school, and I wrote him to let him know that if he wanted to attend high school, I would help him. There was no high school in the village and he had to go to Mouzaki. Finally he decided to go to high school in Mouzaki and stayed with a family from our village. I sent him thirty dollars every month for rent and food. He continued going to high school for two years, but since he had not interest in school, the principal one day said to him, "Return to your village, Miltiadis! Don't spend your father's earnings for nothing, if you don't want to study." I felt terrible for him not continuing with his studies, because I didn't get the opportunity to go to high school like he had.

I had been in the United States for five years when I applied to be an American citizen. In 1961, I went to the courthouse with George Capetanios. I was nervous while the judge asked me some questions, which I responded to without any difficulty. When I finished, the judge got up, congratulated me and wished me good luck in becoming an American citizen. I was thrilled at having passed the test!

After five years at the same job, they started laying us off since we belonged to a union. My turn came to be unemployed. After being at home for two days, someone came to my aunt's house. He knocked at the door and asked for me. He was from Tsikopi Mills and had received my name from my previous job. He had been told that I was a very good worker, and wanted me to work for them. I responded that I would be at the new job the next day. The Tsikopi Mills were located

49

on the other side of the Merrimack River, not very far from my house. They gave me one hundred thirty small looms that made gauzes. I knew my job well, and I didn't have any problems.

My problems started when I had to send all of my money to Greece. My brother Nicholas owned a store and since the people didn't have any money, he allowed them to buy things on credit. When he went to Mouzaki to borrow money for his store from Mitsio Theologi, he sent me a letter to pay for his loans. I wrote to him to close down the store since he was losing money. The problem with my brother Nicholas bothered me a lot, and I couldn't sleep due to my nerves. I visited the doctor for my ailments and he couldn't find anything wrong with me.

In1962, I received a letter from my father stating that my sister Konstantia was of age to get married. At that time in order to get married to an educated person, the bride had to give gold coins as dowry. Since my parents had only one daughter, they wanted to marry her to an educated man. I loved my parents a lot because they had suffered so much to support their five boys and girl, especially during the difficult years of the Greek Civil War. Many times they gave their share of food to their children. They brought up all their children with love and respect. Thus, I responded to my father that if they found an educated husband for Konstantia, they should notify me.

Marriage back then was only by matchmaking. George Apostolou from the village of Leontito came to ask for my sister's hand. He was a teacher and asked for three thousand dollars as dowry. My parents had the engagement party and then they wrote to me asking me to send them the money or there would be no wedding. I had managed to save one thousand dollars that I had in the bank. I had to borrow two thousand dollars more to come up with the three thousand dollars for my sister's dowry. I managed to come up with the amount and sent a check to my father for three thousand dollars for my sister's wedding. The wedding took place as soon as they received the money. My parents, my sister and brother-in-law were very happy and at the same time very proud of me. Later, they became parents of two sons and a daughter. When George, my brother-in-law, turned fifty-five, he was able to retire as a teacher. One day he didn't feel too well and visited the doctor who diagnosed him with cancer. He died at the age of fifty-five just as he began his retirement. He was a very nice person and a good father and husband.

I continued with the same job. Besides not having money, I still owed two thousand dollars at the bank. In February, my friend Charlie Mirmingis, told me to take some time off to go with him to Florida. I didn't have a clue where Florida was and neither did I know anything about the state. Charlie was afraid to travel by plane so we took the train to Florida. We left Manchester in the middle of the winter leaving behind much snow and severe winds only to arrive after thirty-six hours to a warm climate in Lake Worth in Florida. The place was beautiful, covered with flowers, green grass and a temperature of eighty-two degrees. Right away, I fell in love with Florida and I said to my friend Charlie that one of these days I would move to this place. We had a wonderful time there.

In the spring, I was thinking of looking for a better job because the hourly rate was always the same at the mill. My friend Charlie had a restaurant at York Beach in Maine, which he opened on Mother's Day and closed it on Columbus Day, in October.

If I had stayed in Manchester, my future would not have changed. I would never have learned the language due to the large Greek population, the Greek coffee houses, playing horses, and playing cards. That is why one day; I knocked at the door of my boss, Mr. Hosfall. He invited me in and told me to sit down. When I told him about my life and that I wanted to look for a better job with more money, he was very understanding. I gave my three weeks notice, before leaving the mill. I begged him to leave an open door for me, in case I had to come back if I was not very successful in finding a better job. He got up, shook my hand and told me that the door would always be open if I wanted to return. It is very difficult to meet people like Mr. Hosfall. He was so kind and understanding. I will never forget him!

Thus, I left the mill and went to work in the Restaurant in Maine. It was June and vacation time for everyone. The business at the restaurant was horrible. One day we made only sixteen dollars and my friend Charlie was mad and upset and started to scream. The Restaurant had many problems: it didn't have a good parking area, good signage, no air-condition and did not sell hard liquor. I told my friend that he had to fix all of the above if he wanted to be successful. He was able to make the changes, but he still needed a bartender. Finally, I persuaded him to serve beer and wine in the restaurant. The work started to pick up and the restaurant made more than thirty thousand dollars that summer. In 1963 he started serving whiskey at the restaurant. Since we couldn't find a bartender, I took the book 'Mr. Boston', and began to learn how to become a bartender. Now, the work at the restaurant was going very well and I worked seven days a week without any vacation.

On top of the restaurant, Charlie had a room where I slept. The money I was earning was not enough, but since I didn't have the time to go anywhere to spend it, it accumulated. At the same time, I learned the job of bartending.

In the summer of 1963, I received a letter from my father that he wasn't feeling very well. My father had lived a very difficult life. When he was a soldier in 1912, he went to fight against the Turks and the Bulgarians in order to free Greece. He told me that when he was fighting in Kavala with three thousand Greek soldiers, they tried not to be captured by the Turks. They found boats and went to sea. They were at sea for three days when a German ship picked them up and took them to Germany, where they incarcerated them. Since the Germans didn't have a lot of food to feed them, they made bread with a little bit of flour and a lot of sawdust. When one of the soldiers died of starvation, they threw him in one of the spring water fountains, which they used for drinking. The rest of them were workers, making roads and doing different kind of jobs. They were prisoners of war and weren't allowed to return to Greece. After three years, they set them free to return to their country. My father spent three years in Germany and three years in the Greek Army, a total of six years. Upon his return to his village, he got married and had a family. He had smoked since he was twenty-one years old, and when he got older he began to drink. The doctors diagnosed him with cancer of the esophagus and on December 15, 1963, he died at the age of seventy-three. I felt sorry at not being able to go to see him for the last time, because I respected and loved him, and I always listened to him.

In May of 1964 when Charlie opened up the restaurant again, he also put breakfast on the menu and told me to take orders from the customers. I told him that I didn't know how to write English. The first day, when I took my first order, my customer wanted coffee. I was very nervous! My hands trembled as I carried the cup of coffee. It made such a noise that one could hear it from a mile away. The noise was like that of galloping horses on the paved road. Later, we had waitresses when the work picked up and I, on the other hand, felt more comfortable taking orders. The menu had numbers and prices. When I took the order, I wrote only the number and not the words, and took them to the kitchen where I explained the order in Greek to my friend. When I gave the check to my customers I used to hide because I was ashamed of the check, which was only numbers and the price. Of course they didn't mind it since they knew that I didn't know any English. The tips were very good since I was always willing to walk an extra mile to make my customers happy.

Thus, another summer slipped away. In October when we closed the restaurant, I returned to Manchester, staying with my aunt and uncle. In the wintertime I spent three to four weeks in Florida where I became acquainted with some people. There was a very nice restaurant where I often used to eat called The Famous Restaurant. The owners were from Czechoslovakia. The father's name was Jery Broz and they had two children: Edward and Jack.

They became my friends. I told them the following year that I would stay in Florida for three to four months and I would need a job. Their answer was that upon my return to Florida, I would have a job in their restaurant.

I returned once more to Manchester. During that time I didn't have a steady job for the whole year. From Greece, I received letters and everyone was doing fine. I was worried however about my mother who was getting old and I had promised her that I would visit her soon. I had missed all of them especially my country. My mother always wrote to me that I helped them so much and was happy that things got better with my help. Her only wish for me was to find a nice lady to marry, so I wouldn't be all alone in my old age in a foreign land. I always told her not to worry because everything was coming along fine.

Summer came and the restaurant opened again. Charlie was very happy because business was very good. I made good money for the first time in my life, and I went to get my driver's license, but I had not bought a car yet.

At the end of October, I left again for Florida. I met my friends, the Broz family, who gave me work at their restaurant. I worked part-time at the bar, from eleven in the evening until four o'clock in the morning. At the same time, we served sandwiches at the bar but I couldn't write English. One nice lady who had her own restaurant helped me by giving me a paper with all the names of the sandwiches, and by looking at the list, I wrote the order. This was like school to me. I was very happy and I loved my customers. Every day the girls from the bank would come for their lunch. I think that they liked my accent that is why they came very often to our place.

My boss told me that if a customer ordered four drinks the fifth one was to be free. There was a lady by the name of Margie who after two drinks wanted to get the next one free. I told her that only after four drinks, would she get the next one free, but she still continued her nagging. This bothered me a lot. One day I got mad. I paid out of my pocket for her free drinks. After that incident, she never asked for a free drink after her second one. One day instead of forty dollars, I rang four hundred dollars into the register. Right away I informed my boss about my mistake but he told me not to worry because ever since I started working there, he was making two hundred dollars more than he made previously. It pleased me a lot that he was making more money, since I had started working there.

It was a beautiful day. Edward and I were having a conversation when all of a sudden; he asked me if I had a car. I told him that I did have a license but I didn't have enough money to purchase a car. He then told me about a car owned by a lady who had died and owed thirty-five dollars to her lawyer. I thought that I didn't have anything to lose and I gave her lawyer thirty five dollars. He in return gave me the papers and the keys for the car. I went to start the engine right away and it started. I turned the wheel to go forward and it went backward. I turned on the radio. It was working well, and I was able to hear the news from the United States and even from Cuba. Then, I said to myself, "For thirty-five dollars that I gave what do you expect".

One of the customers where I worked asked me why I was so happy. He had never seen me sad. I replied to him, "Why should I be sad? I have no money or house. I have a job, and I have a car that I bought for thirty-five dollars." He was surprised when he heard that I had bought a car for thirty-five dollars. Then, I told him the whole story about my car. He laughed so much that he fell on the floor.

In the month of December when my friend Charlie came from Manchester, I had fixed my car but it still needed more work. For the first time, we went to the dog races in West Palm Beach. My friend was driving the car. When he turned the wheel to the right or to the left, the horn was activated and we couldn't stop it. Naturally, people looked at us to find out what was happening. As they watched us, I waved at them. I pretended that I knew them. The truth was that the car served me well for the time that I lived in Florida that year. At the end of my stay, I sold it for seventy-five dollars when I returned to Manchester.

I returned to Maine for the summer and in the winter I went to Florida. In 1966, my friend Charlie told me that he had a girlfriend in Keene New Hampshire that he had known since high school and was going to ask her to marry him. On April 20, a Greek dance was taking place in Keene and we went to meet his girlfriend, Marina. Marina had a sister Jennie Kazanas. I liked her a lot but I didn't have money or a good job. I was forty years old then. I went out for one year and a half with Jennie. I was in love with her. In 1967, Charlie got married to Marina. In 1968, I started working at Sanders Electronic Company in Manchester. I was making two dollars an hour. That was it. There was no hope for me to get a raise. At the same time, I bought a car: *Ford Sport Coupe*, for $2,400 dollars. In May of the same year, my relationship with Jennie ended because there was no money to get married and start a family. But, we always remained good friends. The summer was over and we closed the restaurant in October and in November, I left for Florida. Up until February of 1969, I had nothing. I was depressed as I saw a dark cloud in my future. All of my friends asked me why I wasn't working and I told them that I couldn't find a job. Then a friend of mine, Joe Green, told me that he knew of a nice place for me to get a job, where he worked part time. He wanted a full time job and the part time job that he had would be ideal for me. It was a good job working for six months in Florida and six months in Maine. Suddenly, I said to myself that there was no need to be depressed. There was always hope for my future.

Finally, I decided to go where my friend worked and asked for a job. I was forty-two years old. The club was called Gulf Stream Bath and Tennis Club. I found the manager, Andre Stevens, and I asked if I could be a bartender for his club. He said that he already had a bartender but I could start as a busboy and if there was an opening, he would consider me for that position. The club opened the first of November and closed in May. It was an ideal job for me.

Spiros at work at the Club: *Gulf Stream Bath and Tennis Club*

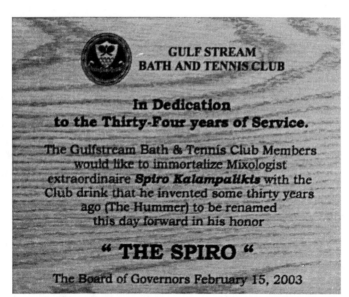

This club was luxurious. It had four hundred thirty nine members and all of them were very kind and educated. My job was difficult, but I had hoped that the manager would see that I was a hard worker and would give me the opportunity to be a bartender, a job that I loved the most! I was never afraid to talk to the members. I was always on time, and I never took any time off. I was taking care of the tables by bringing water, butter, spoons, and forks to the members and whatever else they needed. When the place closed, my boss told me that he liked my work and the crew was satisfied with the service that I had offered. With a smile, he told me that I could have the job as a bartender the following year. They used to call me *"Greek Boy"*. All of the customers were seventy years old and above.

I left for New Hampshire. My job was waiting for me in Maine. I received letters very often from Greece. My mother was waiting to see me. My brother Nicholas had four boys: Anestis was three years old when I left Greece in 1956. Christos came next then Aristitidis and the last one was Ilias, named after my father. Since we had relatives in Athens, the three oldest boys went to live in Athens. They worked in the daytime and went to school at night.

In October of 1969, when my job was over in Maine, I was very happy to be returning to Florida to work as a bartender. At the beginning, Andre kept a close eye on what I was doing, but after a while he was happy with my work and left me alone. I worked very hard and I made sure that the bar was spotless. I had observed that my customers were happy with the drinks that I was making and always said the best things about me to Andre. Now I had a job that I loved and became a very good worker.

I settled down, and having a good job I started to save money because I wanted to go back to Greece. I had missed everyone. Finally in 1972, I decided to visit Greece. I applied for my American passport and I was very proud that I was traveling as an American citizen. On the first of June, I bought my ticket with T.W.A. Airlines. I had to stop in Rome and from there to Athens. I had already written to my uncle Yianni Kartalis and to my nephews about the day of my arrival in Athens. When I was packing my suitcase, my uncle George tied a red and blue ribbon to the handles of the suitcase. When I asked him why he was doing that, he said that it was a good way to recognize my luggage at the airport, so I would not lose time looking for them. My uncle had never traveled but he was a wise man.

I left from New York to Rome. When we arrived in Rome, the airport workers were on strike and didn't bother to help us at all. They took all the luggage from the airplane and put them in a small room outside the airport. The passengers started to scream. I went to look for my suitcases and it was a good thing that my uncle had tied the ribbons around the handles. I was able to find them in no time. I had a half an hour to catch the next flight to Athens. I asked the airport officials for the gate to Athens, but they didn't bother to help me. Finally, exhausted and stressed out, I approached the ticket counter and began to speak to them in Greek. I told them that I was Greek and begged them to take me to the gate for Athens. I think that they felt sorry for me and helped me until I was on the airplane. Within ten minutes, the airplane took off for Athens. I was lucky! After two hours, we entered the Greek territory from Dodekanisos and headed for Athens. I was thrilled to be back in Greece, my native land. Next to me was seated a very nice lady that I was constantly talking to, telling her that I had not visited Greece for sixteen years, and that is why I was so happy to see the airplane descending. I told her, "Open the window so I can jump out. I can't wait for the airplane to touch the Greek soil. She replied, "Don't do that! No...No...No.!"

Finally, we were at the airport in Athens. My nephews were waiting for me, but since they didn't recognized me, I took a taxi to go to the section called Zografos in Athens, where my uncle Kartalis lived and was waiting for me. When I arrived at his house, my nephews called my uncle to tell him that I was nowhere to be seen. Then, my uncle told them that I was already in his house and to return home. Within half an hour, I met and got acquainted with my nephews.

The following day when I woke up, the sun was shining, Greek music was playing everywhere, and everybody was speaking Greek. It was right there and then, that I started to believe that I was truly and finally in my nostalgic beautiful country of Greece. I went to visit my nephews. They lived in a small room. They worked hard during the day and attended school at night. I congratulated them on their hard work and told them that there were no doubts in my mind that they would be successful in the future.

The second day, the brother of my aunt, my uncle Thomas Kourtis with his wife, Effie Kartali and my nephew Anestis and I went to Plaka to hear the bouzoukia. It was customary in those days to break dishes when one danced. I always loved music and dancing. They had music from different parts of Greece and I asked them if it was possible for me to dance. When they told me that it was okay, I danced all the dances especially the tsamiko. One of the members of the band complimented me on dancing so well after sixteen years of being away in America. I responded that one never forgets the Greek customs and dances. They are rooted in the soul. I didn't break dishes that night. I only threw dollars at the band and I thanked them for allowing me to dance.

After three days, I left for my village. I took the bus to Arta. I wanted to visit Corintho, Antirio, Mesolongi and Agrinion. My brother Nicholas was waiting for me in Arta. As soon as we met, we went to visit the village Kompoti, where we had stayed for three years as refugees, during the Greek Civil War. I had not been back there for twenty-two years. We met with some of our friends especially Mrs. Koulouli where we stayed for three years without paying any rent. Mr. Koulouli had died two years previously. She had three daughters and a son. Upon thanking his wife for their help during the most difficult years of our lives, we left for the village.

Mrs. Koulouli and Nicholas Kalampalikis

When we arrived at the village, my mother embraced me and kissed me for ten minutes without letting me go. The relatives and villagers asked me about life in the United States. Life in the village had changed a lot since my departure. Everyone was working and the government was helping to build roads in the mountains in northern part of Greece. The saddest thing for me was that I didn't see my father. He had died as had the other elderly people in the village. The days flew by and soon I had to return to America. My mother constantly told me to get married so I wouldn't be alone in a foreign land. Finally I left for Athens. I said good-bye to Greece and left for America.

Spiros' Mother: Paraskevi Kalampalikis

I was satisfied with my trip. I took a lot of pictures of the village and special parts of Greece for my uncle and aunt who had not visited Greece since 1915.

My uncle and aunt were waiting for me to tell them all the news from Greece. My uncle asked me about all the places in the village. He still remembered every corner, every place of the village. I told them that I went to the mountain called Klokovos. It was adorned with pine trees and all the hills were covered with wild flowers. I inhaled the freshest air and the most aromatic scent of nature. I saw tears rolling from my uncle's eyes. It was evident that he had missed his village.

I went to Florida where I continued with my work at the club. Everyone liked me and treated me very well. In May of 1974, they gave me a bonus of $3,500 dollars, which for me was a lot of money.

My main goal was to find a nice girl to marry, because I was getting tired of living alone. In America, I had met many girls, not counting

Jennie, but I never took the special step to get married. Many of them were older and others younger than me.

In July 1976, I left for Greece. I had only four weeks off. I went to my village to see my mother and my brothers, but I didn't say anything to them of wanting to get married. I looked at the village girls. All of them were too young and I was a forty-eight year old man. Secondly, I didn't want to get married by matchmaking. For me love is something that is rooted deep in the heart and lasts for many years. The time came for me to leave. When I said good-bye to my mother, I felt that that would be the last time that I would have the opportunity to see her, to embrace her because she was very old and her health was deteriorating. With those sad thoughts, I returned to America.

In 1977, in Delray Beach, Florida, I bought a house, which was three miles away from my job. I couldn't control my happiness. I started fixing the house. I wanted everything to be perfect. The same year, my brother Tom and Lazaros sent the papers to my brother Nicholas to come to the United States for six months so he could bring his children here. When I went back to Maine, I met my brother Nicholas and I asked him how he liked America. He told me that it was one of the best countries in the world, but as soon as his children came to America, he would return to Greece. Besides, someone had to stay in the village to look after our mother in her old age.

I returned to Florida to work and to see my house. In 1978, I finished my work and went to Lake Worth to visit the Broz family. There, I saw for the first time a beautiful young lady who was working as a hostess. She gave me the menu with a smile. I didn't pay attention to her the first time. When I went back the second time, I asked her if she was married. She told me that she was divorced. I asked her for a date and she accepted. We went to a very nice restaurant to eat and to become better acquainted. Her name was Darlene and she had a twelve-year-old son, Scott. She was born in Woodstock, Ontario, Canada. Her parents were John and Kathleen Forrest. Due to the health problems her father had with asthma, the doctors advised him to move to a place with better climate. Thus, they came to West Palm Beach in 1957 when Darlene was fifteen years old. We went out for six months and finally we got married on September 16, 1978. For our honeymoon, we went to New Hampshire so that Darlene could meet my family. When we arrived in Manchester, my nephew Anestis had arrived from Greece to live in the United States. We had a wonderful time.

In 1979 we were unable to go to Greece as I had promised my mother. My mother died on October 12, 1979, at the age of 85. From that point on, I had no interest in returning to Greece.

On August 20, 1981, my uncle died from old age at the age of 94. My uncle was a hard working man who worked in a tannery for forty years until he retired at the age of 74. He helped all of my siblings and I, sending us money in the village. Two years later, on September 12, 1983, my aunt Anastasia died. For me, they were my second parents. I had lived in their house from 1956 until the day that my aunt died.

It was 1988 when my wife Darlene and I decided to visit Greece. We bought the tickets so I could show my wife my native village, where I spent my youthful years. We left with a British Airline and stopped in London where we stayed for four days. London is a very nice city. I liked to hear the English people speaking and to watch the way they were dressed up for their jobs, in nice-clean outfits. This brought back memories of the British lieutenants who came to our village during the Greek Civil War.

After four days, we left for Greece, where my nephew Christos was waiting for us. He took us to the Avenue Papagos where he lived. We were going to stay with him. Christos had attended the University, and out of 14,000 students was 314 in his class. It was Darlene's first time in Athens. We visited the outdoor market where there was an abundance of fruit and vegetables. She became intoxicated with everything that she was seeing.

It was the first time that we went to the village by car. Naturally the road was not paved. My brother, Nicholas was waiting for us there with my sister-in-law, Georgia. It would have been more pleasurable if my mother was alive to meet Darlene, but unfortunately she had passed away. I showed Darlene all the places in my village where we grew up, and told her about the difficult years that we lived through during the Greek Civil War. She liked the village life, and the nature, but most of all she loved the people.

From the village, we left for Arta, Preveza and Lefkada. We stayed three days in Lefkada where at that time we felt the rumblings of a small earthquake. It was Darlene's first time to experience an earthquake. From afar we saw the island of Skorpios where Onassis used to live.

Our trip came to an end and it was time for us to return to Athens. My beloved Darlene loved Greece and didn't want to leave. She cried on the way back to the United States.

We returned to America. The year passed by so fast! My family was separated, half in Greece and half in the United States. The three sons of my brother Nicholas came to America and became American citizens and eventually became the owners of three restaurants. They got married and had their own families. The oldest, Anestis, married Angeliki and had two children, Nicholas and Gena. Aristidis married Effie and the youngest one, Ilias, married Angeliki and had a son George. I congratulate them all for their hard work and their successes. They took advantage of all the opportunities that the United States had to offer.

I continued working at the club. In 2002, I began to think of retirement. I wrote a letter to the committee of the club telling them that I wanted to retire. At the same time I wanted to continue working part time at the club because I knew that I would miss my job. They didn't have any objections. Thus, after thirty-four years of having a good job at the club and being in good health, I retired at the age of 75.

I spent 48 wonderful years in the United States. I didn't become rich but I am not poor. I am very satisfied with my accomplishments since arriving in New York with only eight dollars in my pocket.

GOD BLESS AMERICA THE LAND OF EQUALITY, LIBERTY AND OPPORTUNITY FOR ALL!

This is the famous Bridge of Arta. The story goes that the men built it during the day, and at night it would crumble. This went on for weeks until the architect saw in a dream a woman dressed in black telling him that he had to bury his wife in the foundation if he wanted to complete the bridge. The next day, he buried his wife alive in the bridge. Finally, the construction of the bridge was finished. They say that the bridge still shakes, even today, due to his wife's screams.

The Bridge of Arta

1. Reunion after thirty-one years in New York. From left to right: Spiros Kalampalikis, Demetrios Teligadas, and Chrisostomos Pouzios.

2. Spiros' wife Darlene, the priest of Argiri, Lambro Karanikas with his grandchildren, and a boy by the last name of Panagiotou. .

3-4. Mother and Father: Paraskevi and Elias Kalampalikis.

Mr. and Mrs. Elias Kalampalikis

5. Spiros with his four brothers and sister. From left to right: Nicholas, Spiros, Konstantia, Tom, Lazaros and Miltiadis.

6. Parent's tomb in the village.

7. House in Prava that Spiros lived in when he was three years old.

The Epilogue

As I approach the sunset of my life, I go back to revisit my long journey. What a journey that has been!

Although my struggles started when I was a small child, born in a small village in Thessali, Greece, I traveled and visited places and met people that I never dreamed that I would have the opportunity to meet or see. How can anyone have any regrets after having a journey like mine? My failures, struggles, sufferings and starvation were the best teachers in my life, bringing forth success and beautiful memories that I will always cherish.

Yes indeed, I am a very lucky man! I was blessed with lots of love from my parents, my siblings, nephews and above all from my wonderful wife who stood like a rock, next to me, through the successful and happy days of our lives, living in the beautiful country, the United States of America.

ISBN 142511059-2